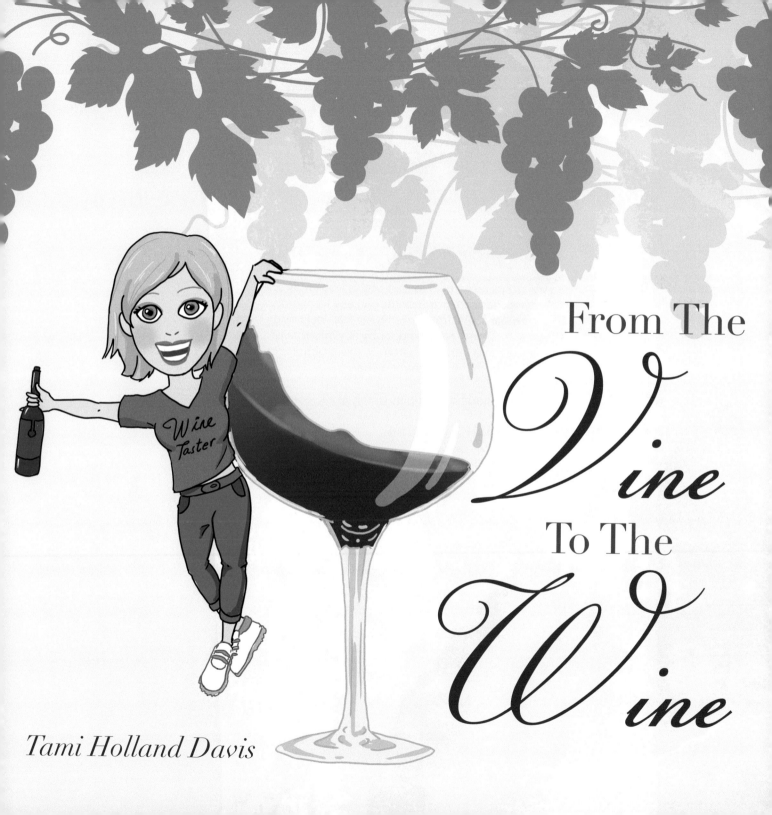

From The
Vine
To The
Wine

Tami Holland Davis

To order additional copies of this book, contact:
Xlibris
844-714-8691
www.Xlibris.com
Orders@Xlibris.com

ISBN: Softcover   978-1-6641-8887-7
        EBook   978-1-6641-8886-0

Print information available on the last page

Rev. date: 08/06/2021

From The Vine To The Wine

OFFICIAL

WINE TASTER

I saved some *WINE* today. It was trapped in a

Bottle

THE ANSWER
MAY NOT LIE
AT THE
BOTTOM OF
A BOTTLE
OF WINE.
BUT YOU SHOULD
AT LEAST CHECK.

Red Wine

oh look
-it's-
wine
o'clock

How I tell time....

AM   PM

Beans or Grapes

One Winery Tour
Two Wineree Toor
Tree Winry Twoor
FLOOR!

Men are like fine wine.

They all start out like grapes
and it's our job to stomp on them
and keep them in the dark until
they mature into something
you'd like to have dinner with

W.I.N.O.S.
Women in Need of Sanity

A real friend
Knows when to listen
When to stop listening,
When to talk,
When to stop talking,
When to pour wine,
When to stop pouring –
And just hand over
the bottle.

dear WINE,
we had a deal.
you were to make me funnier, sexier, smarter and a better dancer.
i saw the video.
we need to talk.

GIVE ME *Coffee* **to Change** THE THINGS I CAN & *Wine* to accept the things **I CANNOT**

WINE FOR EVERYONE!

GROUP THERAPY

WINE IS LIFE

TAMI   KAT   MELODY   SHARON   KRISTI

Learn the Five S's of
WINE TASTING

1 SWIRL ———————————————

2 SNIFF ———

3 SLURP ———————————————

4 SWISH ———

5 SWALLOW ———————————

PAIRING

Cabernet Sauvignon
&
Extra Sharp Cheddar

Chardonnay
&
Parmesan

Merlot
&
Gouda

Pinot Noir
&
Brie

Malbec
&
Vintage/Reserve Cheese

Sauvignon Blanc
&
Feta

Wine Tasting Notes

Name	Winery	Vintage	Rating	Comments
1			1 2 3 4 5 6 7 8 9 10	
2			1 2 3 4 5 6 7 8 9 10	
3			1 2 3 4 5 6 7 8 9 10	
4			1 2 3 4 5 6 7 8 9 10	
5			1 2 3 4 5 6 7 8 9 10	
6			1 2 3 4 5 6 7 8 9 10	
7			1 2 3 4 5 6 7 8 9 10	
8			1 2 3 4 5 6 7 8 9 10	
9			1 2 3 4 5 6 7 8 9 10	
10			1 2 3 4 5 6 7 8 9 10	
11			1 2 3 4 5 6 7 8 9 10	
12			1 2 3 4 5 6 7 8 9 10	

ONCE UPON A TIME
THERE WAS A
WOMAN WHO
REALLY NEEDED
A BIG GLASS
OF WINE

IT WAS ME
THE END

Printed in the United States
by Baker & Taylor Publisher Services